3

american popular piano

ETUDES

Compositions by
Christopher Norton

Additional Compositions and Arrangements
Dr. Scott McBride Smith

Editor
Dr. Scott McBride Smith

Associate Editors

Clarke MacIntosh

Dr. Richard Holbrook

Book Design & Engraving
Andrew Jones

Cover Design
Wagner Design

A Note about this Book

Pop music styles can be grouped into three broad categories:

- **lyrical** — pieces with a beautiful singing quality and rich harmonies; usually played at a slow tempo;

- **rhythmic** — more up-tempo pieces, with energetic, catchy rhythms; these often have a driving left hand part;

- **ensemble** — works meant to be played with other musicians, or with backing tracks (or both!); this type of piece requires careful listening and shared energy.

American Popular Piano has been deliberately designed to develop skills in all three areas.

You can integrate the cool, motivating pieces in **American Popular Piano** into your piano studies in several ways.

- pick a piece you like and learn it; when you're done, pick another!

- choose a piece from each category to develop a complete range of skills in your playing;

- polish a particular favorite for your local festival or competition. Works from **American Popular Piano** are featured on the lists of required pieces for many festivals and competitions;

- use the pieces as optional contemporary selections in music examinations;

- Or...just have fun!

Going hand-in-hand with the repertoire in **American Popular Piano** are the innovative **Etudes Albums** and **Skills Books**, designed to enhance each student's musical experience by building technical and aural skills.

- **Technical Etudes** in both Classical and Pop Styles are based on musical ideas and technical challenges drawn from the repertoire. Practice these to improve your chops!

- **Improvisation Etudes** offer an exciting new approach to improvisation that guides students effortlessly into spontaneous creativity. Not only does the user-friendly module structure integrate smoothly into traditional lessons, it opens up a whole new understanding of the repertoire being studied.

- **Skills Books** help students develop key supporting skills in sight-reading, ear-training and technic; presented in complementary study modules that are both practical and effective.

Use all of the elements of **American Popular Piano** together to incorporate a comprehensive course of study into your everyday routine. The carefully thought-out pacing makes learning almost effortless. Making music and real progress has never been so much fun!

Library and Archives Canada Cataloguing in Publication

Norton, Christopher, 1953-

American popular piano [music] : etudes / compositions by Christopher Norton ;
additional compositions and arrangements, Scott McBride Smith ;
editor, Scott McBride Smith ; associate editor, S. Clarke MacIntosh.

To be complete in 11 volumes.
The series is organized in 11 levels, from preparatory to level 10, each including a repertoire album,
an etudes album, a skills book, and an instrumental backings compact disc.

ISBN 1-897379-11-0 (preparatory level).--ISBN 1-897379-12-9 (level 1).--
ISBN 1-897379-13-7 (level 2).--ISBN 1-897379-14-5 (level 3).--
ISBN 1-897379-15-3 (level 4).--ISBN 1-897379-16-1 (level 5)

1. Piano--Studies and exercises. I. Smith, Scott McBride II. MacIntosh, S. Clarke, 1959- III. Title.

LEVEL ③ ETUDES
Table of Contents

Improv Etude - War Dance

MODULE 1

A Clap this rhythmic pattern with the backing track:

B Create your own RH melodies, as guided in steps 1-3.
Play without the backing track.
Where improv is indicated:

1. Use scale degree 1.
2. Use scale degrees 5 or 1.
3. Use scale degrees 5, 7, 1, or 2.

C Repeat steps B1-3 with LH accompaniments.

1. Improvise on this rhythm using scale degrees 5, 7, 1, or 2.

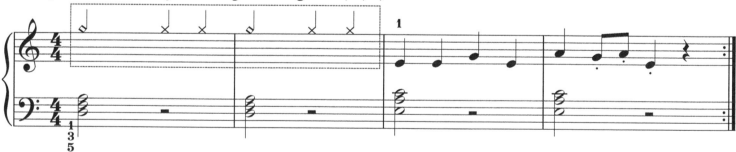

2. Improvise on this rhythm using scale degrees 5, 7, 1, or 2.

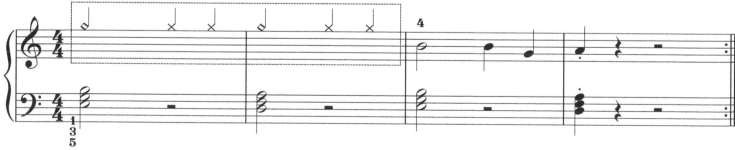

3. Improvise on this rhythm using scale degrees 5, 7, 1, or 2.

* Improv notes:

D Practice hands together with the backing track.
For mm.1-2, 5-6, 9-10, & 13-14 improvise your own
melodies using the given rhythms and your ideas from step "C".

* Improvise:

Listen closely as you play your improvisation.
  - Does each note sound good with the backing track?
  - Are you keeping a steady beat and staying with the backing track?
Play several different improvisations and choose your favorite. Play it for your teacher.

✔ **Improv Tip:** *Make the melody quite marcato (accented) - be war-like!*

Improv Etude - War Dance

MODULE 2

A Clap this rhythmic pattern with the backing track:

B Create your own RH melodies, as guided in steps 1-3.
Play without the backing track.
Where improv is indicated:

1. Use scale degree 1.
2. Use scale degrees 1 or 2.
3. Use scale degrees 1, 2, 3, or 4.

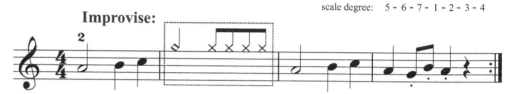

C Repeat steps B1-3 with LH accompaniments.

1. Improvise on this rhythm using scale degrees 1, 2, 3, or 4.

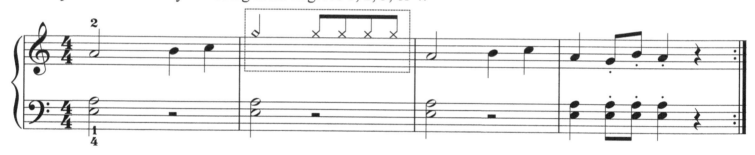

2. Improvise on this rhythm using scale degrees 1, 2, 3, or 4.

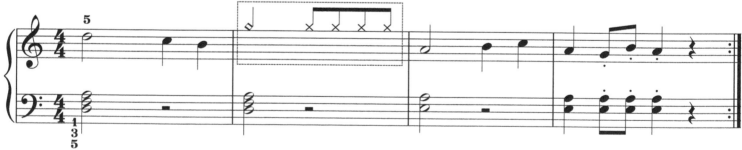

3. Improvise on this rhythm using scale degrees 1, 2, 3, or 4.

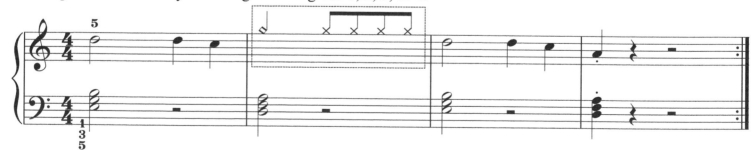

* Improv notes:

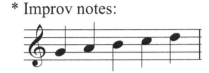

D Practice hands together with the backing track.
For mm. 2, 6, 10, & 14 improvise your own melodies
using the given rhythms and your ideas from step "C".

Listen closely as you play your improvisation.
- Does each note sound good with the backing track?
- Are you keeping a steady beat and staying with the backing track?
Play several different improvisations and choose your favorite. Play it for your teacher.

✔ **Improv Tip:** *Every good melody has a catchy musical idea. What is yours?*

Improv Etude - War Dance

MODULE 3

A Clap this rhythmic pattern with the backing track:

B Create your own RH melodies, as guided in steps 1-3.
Play without the backing track.
Where improv is indicated:

1. Use scale degree 5.
2. Use scale degrees 5 or 1.
3. Use scale degrees 5, 7, 1, 2, or 3.

A Aeolian:

fingering: 1   2

scale degree: 5 - 6 - 7 - 1 - 2 - 3 - 4

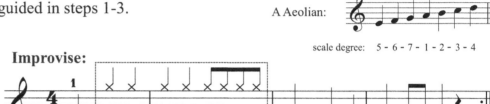

Improvise:

C Repeat steps B1-3 with LH accompaniments.

1. Improvise on this rhythm using scale degrees 5, 7, 1, 2, or 3.

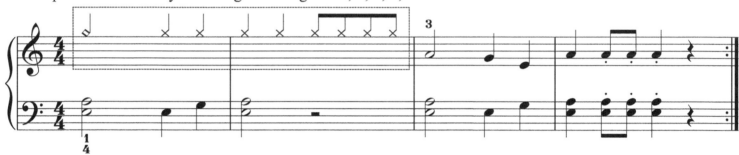

2. Improvise on this rhythm using scale degrees 5, 7, 1, 2, or 3.

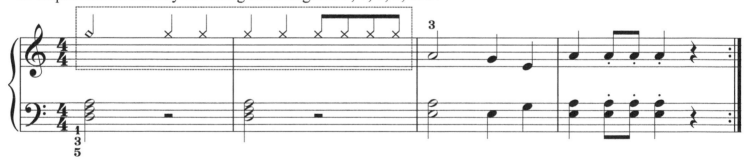

3. Improvise on this rhythm using scale degrees 5, 7, 1, 2, or 3.

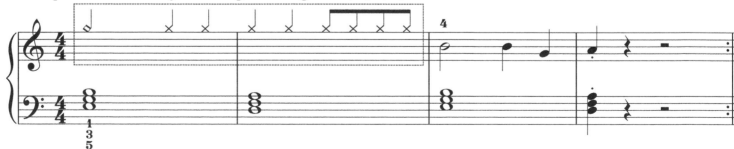

* Improv notes:
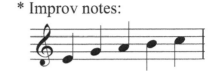

D Practice hands together with the backing track.
For mm.1-2, 5-6, 9-10, & 13-14 improvise your own
melodies using the given rhythms and your ideas from step "C".

* **Improvise:**

Listen closely as you play your improvisation.
- Does each note sound good with the backing track?
- Are you keeping a steady beat and staying with the backing track?
Play several different improvisations and choose your favorite. Play it for your teacher.

✔ **Improv Tip:** *Be adventurous in your choice of notes - there are many to choose from!*

Improv Etude - War Dance

MODULE 4

A Clap this rhythmic pattern with the backing track:

B Create your own RH melodies, as guided in steps 1-3.
Play without the backing track.
Where improv is indicated:

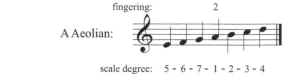

1. Use scale degree 3.
2. Use scale degrees 1 or 3.
3. Use scale degrees 7, 1, 2, 3, or 4.

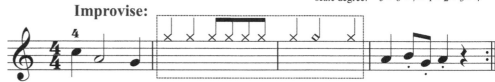

C Repeat steps B1-3 with LH accompaniments.

1. Improvise on this rhythm using scale degrees 7, 1, 2, 3, or 4.

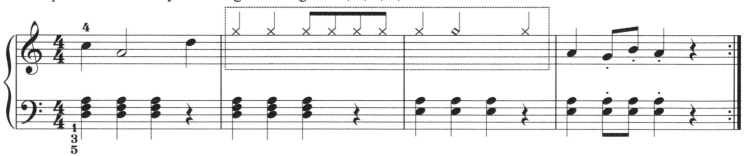

2. Improvise on this rhythm using scale degrees 7, 1, 2, 3, or 4.

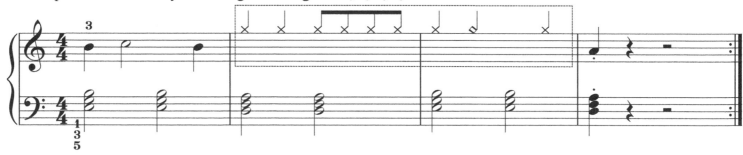

3. Improvise on this rhythm using scale degrees 7, 1, 2, 3, or 4.

* Improv notes:

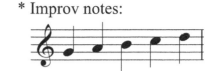

D Practice hands together with the backing track.
For mm.2-3, 6-7, 10-11, & 14-15 improvise your own
melodies using the given rhythms and your ideas from step "C".

Listen closely as you play your improvisation.
  - Does each note sound good with the backing track?
  - Are you keeping a steady beat and staying with the backing track?
Play several different improvisations and choose your favorite. Play it for your teacher.

✔ **Improv Tip:** *The left hand reinforces the main melody notes much of the time.*
      How do you know it is a main note?

Improv Etude - Celtic Caper

MODULE 1

A Clap this rhythmic pattern with the backing track:

B Create your own RH melodies, as guided in steps 1-3.
Play without the backing track.
Where improv is indicated:

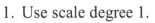

1. Use scale degree 1.
2. Use scale degrees 1 or 3.
3. Use scale degrees 1, 2, 3, 4, or 5.

C Repeat steps B1-3 with LH accompaniments.

1. Improvise on this rhythm using scale degrees 1, 2, 3, 4, or 5.

2. Improvise on this rhythm using scale degrees 7, 1, 2, 3, 4, or 5.

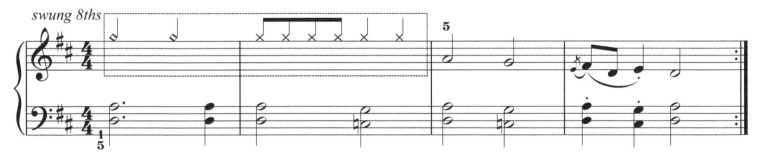

3. Improvise on this rhythm using scale degrees 7, 1, 2, 3, 4, or 5.

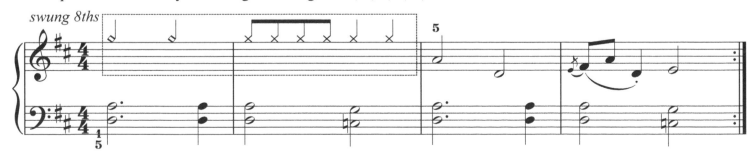

Improv notes:

D Practice hands together with the backing track.
For mm. 2-3, & 5-6 improvise your own melodies
using the given rhythms and your ideas from step "C".

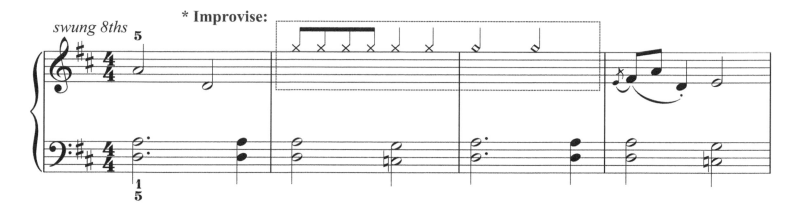

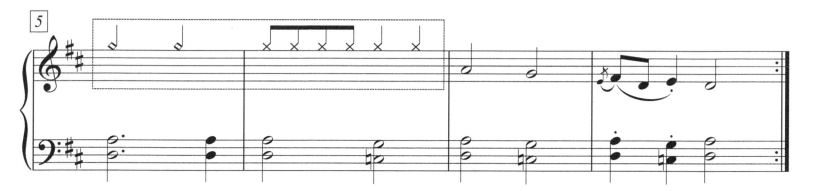

Listen closely as you play your improvisation.
- Does each note sound good with the backing track?
- Are you keeping a steady beat and staying with the backing track?
Play several different improvisations and choose your favorite. Play it for your teacher.

✔ **Improv Tip:** *Use articulation and swung 8ths to create an extroverted feel.*

Improv Etude - Celtic Caper

MODULE 2

A Clap this rhythmic pattern with the backing track:

B Create your own RH melodies, as guided in steps 1-3.
Play without the backing track.
Where improv is indicated:

1. Use scale degree 1.
2. Use scale degrees 1 or 3.
3. Use scale degrees 1, 2, 3, 4, or 5.

Improvise:

C Repeat steps B1-3 with LH accompaniments.

1. Improvise on this rhythm using scale degrees 1, 2, 3, 4, or 5.

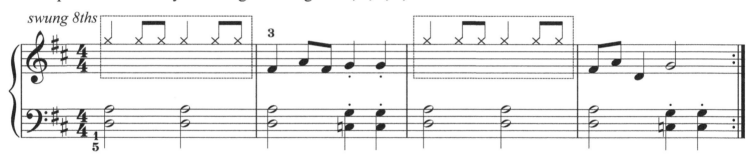

2. Improvise on this rhythm using scale degrees 7, 1, 2, 3, 4, or 5.

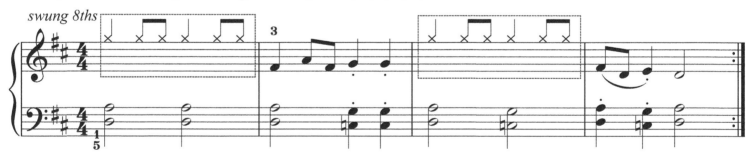

3. Improvise on this rhythm using scale degrees 7, 1, 2, 3, 4, or 5.

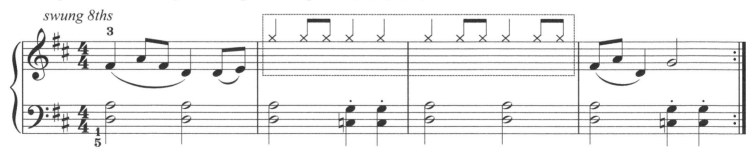

* Improv notes:

D Practice hands together with the backing track.
For mm. 1, 3, 5, & 7 improvise your own melodies
using the given rhythms and your ideas from step "C".

* **Improvise:**

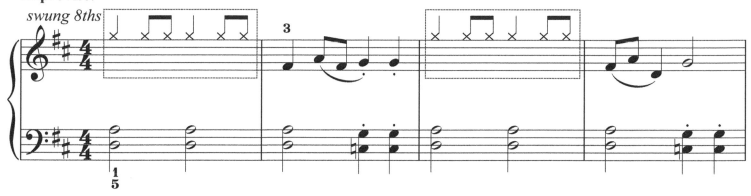

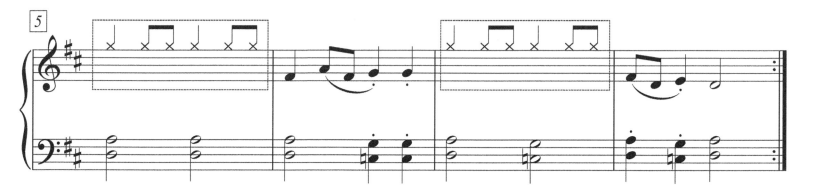

Listen closely as you play your improvisation.
- Does each note sound good with the backing track?
- Are you keeping a steady beat and staying with the backing track?
Play several different improvisations and choose your favorite. Play it for your teacher.

✔ **Improv Tip:** *Going up or down the Improv notes in scale form could be a cool improv.*

Improv Etude - Celtic Caper

MODULE 3

A Clap this rhythmic pattern with the backing track:

B Create your own RH melodies, as guided in steps 1-3.
Play without the backing track.
Where improv is indicated:

1. Use scale degree 1.
2. Use scale degrees 1 or 3.
3. Use scale degrees 1, 2, 3, 4, or 5.

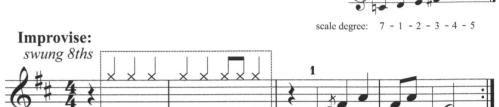

C Repeat steps B1-3 with LH accompaniments.

1. Improvise on this rhythm using scale degrees 1, 2, 3, 4, or 5.

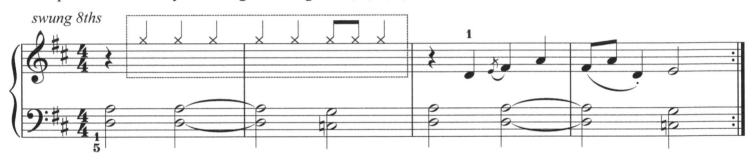

2. Improvise on this rhythm using scale degrees 7, 1, 2, 3, 4, or 5.

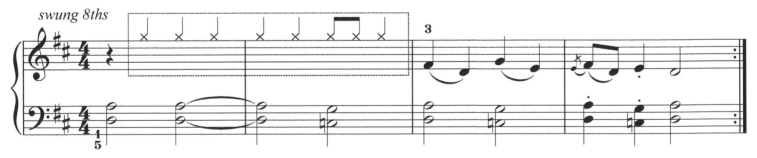

3. Improvise on this rhythm using scale degrees 7, 1, 2, 3, 4, or 5.

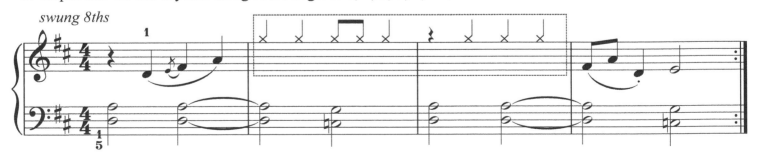

* Improv notes:

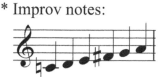

D Practice hands together with the backing track.
For mm. 1-2, & 5-6 improvise your own melodies
using the given rhythms and your ideas from step "C".

* Improvise:
swung 8ths

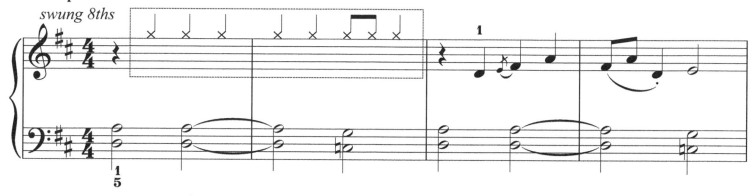

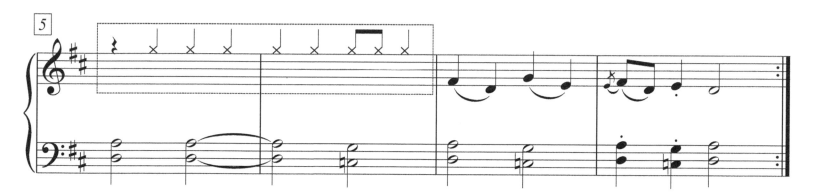

Listen closely as you play your improvisation.
- Does each note sound good with the backing track?
- Are you keeping a steady beat and staying with the backing track?
Play several different improvisations and choose your favorite. Play it for your teacher.

✔ **Improv Tip:** *Try using the Improv notes in scale form - but this time,*
skip one or two and add some repeated notes.

Improv Etude - Celtic Caper

MODULE 4

A Clap this rhythmic pattern with the backing track:

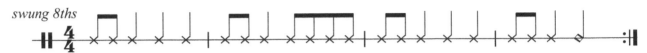

B Create your own RH melodies, as guided in steps 1-3.
Play without the backing track.
Where improv is indicated:

1. Use scale degree 1.
2. Use scale degrees 1 or 3.
3. Use scale degrees 1, 2, 3, 4, or 5.

Improvise:

C Repeat steps B1-3 with LH accompaniments.

1. Improvise on this rhythm using scale degrees 1, 2, 3, 4, or 5.

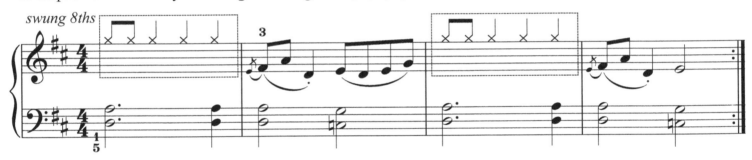

2. Improvise on this rhythm using scale degrees 7, 1, 2, 3, 4, or 5.

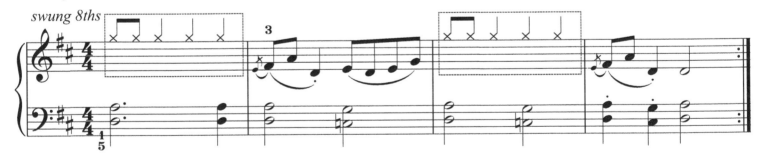

3. Improvise on this rhythm using scale degrees 7, 1, 2, 3, 4, or 5.

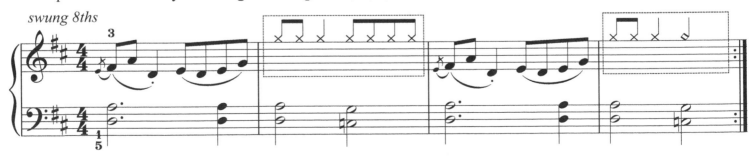

* Improv notes:

D Practice hands together with the backing track.
For mm. 1, 3, 5, & 7 improvise your own melodies
using the given rhythms and your ideas from step "C".

* **Improvise:**

Listen closely as you play your improvisation.
- Does each note sound good with the backing track?
- Are you keeping a steady beat and staying with the backing track?
Play several different improvisations and choose your favorite. Play it for your teacher.

✔ **Improv Tip:** *You can try your improvisation an octave higher when you repeat.*
It will suit the character of the piece.

Improv Etude - KC Shuffle

MODULE 1

A Clap this rhythmic pattern with the backing track:

B Create your own RH melodies, as guided in steps 1-3.
Play without the backing track.
Where improv is indicated:

1. Use scale degree 8.
2. Use scale degrees 5 or 8.
3. Use scale degrees 5, 6, 7, or 8.

fingering: 1

D Mixolydian:

scale degree: 4 - 5 - 6 - 7 - 8

Improvise:

C Repeat steps B1-3 with LH accompaniments.

    1. Improvise on this rhythm using scale degrees 5, 6, 7, or 8.

    2. Improvise on this rhythm using scale degrees 4, 5, 6, 7, or 8.

    3. Improvise on this rhythm using scale degrees 5, 6, 7, or 8.

* Improv notes:

D Practice hands together with the backing track.
For mm. 1, 3, 5, 7, 9 & 11 improvise your own melodies
using the given rhythms and your ideas from step "C".

* **Improvise:**

swung 8ths

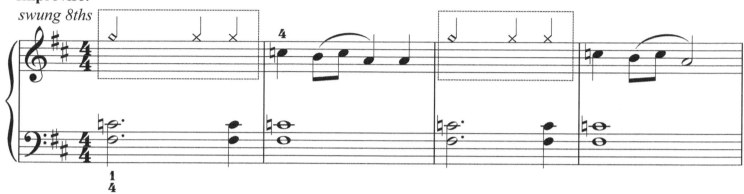

Listen closely as you play your improvisation.
  - Does each note sound good with the backing track?
  - Are you keeping a steady beat and staying with the backing track?
Play several different improvisations and choose your favorite. Play it for your teacher.

✔ **Improv Tip:** *Try putting an accent on any beat of your choice in m. 5.*
            Play the same melody in m. 7, but accent a different beat - the feeling will be different.

Improv Etude - KC Shuffle

MODULE 2

A Clap this rhythmic pattern with the backing track:

B Create your own RH melodies, as guided in steps 1-3.
Play without the backing track.
Where improv is indicated:

1. Use scale degree 8.
2. Use scale degrees 5 or 8.
3. Use scale degrees 5, 6, 7, or 8.

Improvise:

C Repeat steps B1-3 with LH accompaniments.

1. Improvise on this rhythm using scale degrees 5, 6, 7, or 8.

2. Improvise on this rhythm using scale degrees 4, 5, 6, 7, or 8.

3. Improvise on this rhythm using scale degrees 5, 6, 7, or 8.

* Improv notes:

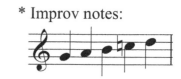

D Practice hands together with the backing track.
For mm. 3-4, 7-8, & 9-10 improvise your own melodies
using the given rhythms and your ideas from step "C".

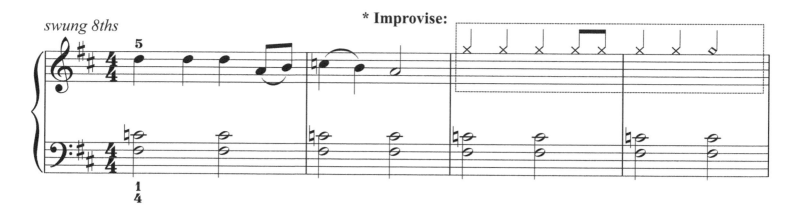

Listen closely as you play your improvisation.
- Does each note sound good with the backing track?
- Are you keeping a steady beat and staying with the backing track?
Play several different improvisations and choose your favorite. Play it for your teacher.

✔ **Improv Tip:** *Try playing a melody in mm. 3-4 that goes up, to contrast the melody in mm. 1-2.*
Now try the same approach in mm. 5-8, with mm. 7-8 going down.

Improv Etude - KC Shuffle

MODULE 3

A Clap this rhythmic pattern with the backing track:

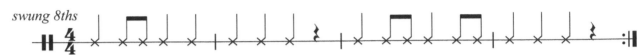

B Create your own RH melodies, as guided in steps 1-3.
Play without the backing track.
Where improv is indicated:

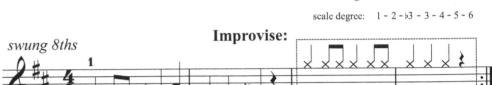

1. Use scale degree 1.
2. Use scale degrees 1 or ♭3.
3. Use scale degrees 1, 2,
   ♭3, 3, 5, or 6.

Improvise:

C Repeat steps B1-3 with LH accompaniments.

1. Improvise on this rhythm using scale degrees 1, 2, ♭3, 3, 5, or 6.

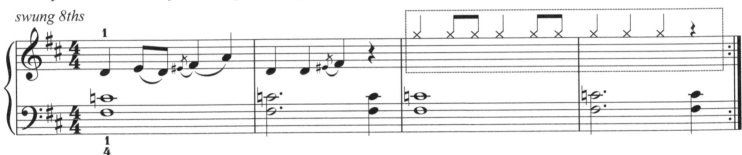

2. Improvise on this rhythm using scale degrees 1, 2, ♭3, 3, 4, 5, or 6.

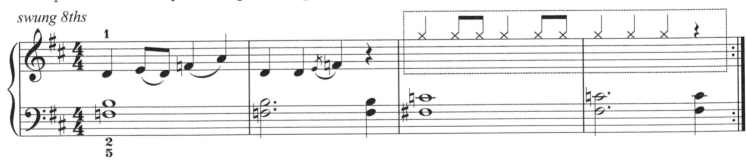

3. Improvise on this rhythm using scale degrees 1, 2, ♭3, 3, 5, or 6.

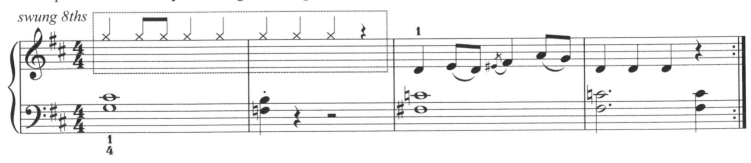

* Improv notes:

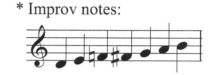

D Practice hands together with the backing track.
For mm. 3-4, 7-8, & 9-10 improvise your own melodies
using the given rhythms and your ideas from step "C".

* Improvise:

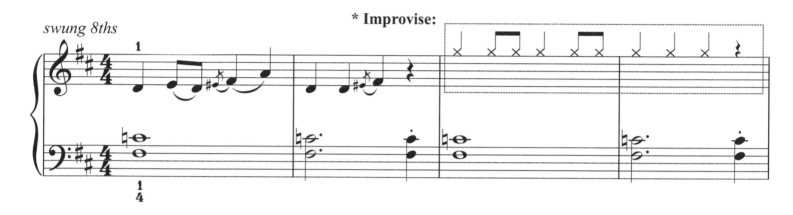

swung 8ths

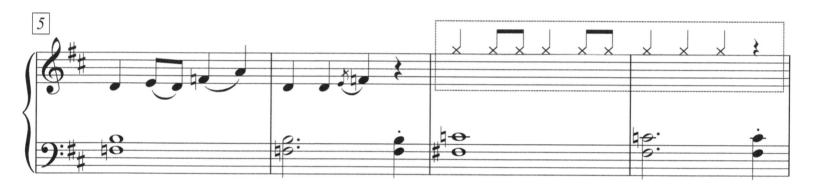

Listen closely as you play your improvisation.
- Does each note sound good with the backing track?
- Are you keeping a steady beat and staying with the backing track?
Play several different improvisations and choose your favorite. Play it for your teacher.

✔ **Improv Tip:** *The "blues notes" sound cool in this piece - the F♮'s "crunch" with the F♯'s.*
Try both notes in your improvisation and enjoy!

Improv Etude - KC Shuffle

MODULE 4

A Clap this rhythmic pattern with the backing track:

B Create your own RH melodies, as guided in steps 1-3.
Play without the backing track.
Where improv is indicated:

1. Use scale degree 1.
2. Use scale degrees 1 or 5.
3. Use scale degrees 1, 2, ♭3, 3, 5, or 6.

C Repeat steps B1-3 with LH accompaniments.

1. Improvise on this rhythm using scale degrees 1, 2, ♭3, 3, 5, or 6.

2. Improvise on this rhythm using scale degrees 1, 2, ♭3, 3, 4, 5, or 6.

3. Improvise on this rhythm using scale degrees 1, 2, ♭3, 3, 5, or 6.

* Improv notes:

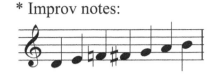

D Practice hands together with the backing track.
For mm. 3-4, 7-8, & 11-12 improvise your own melodies
using the given rhythms and your ideas from step "C".

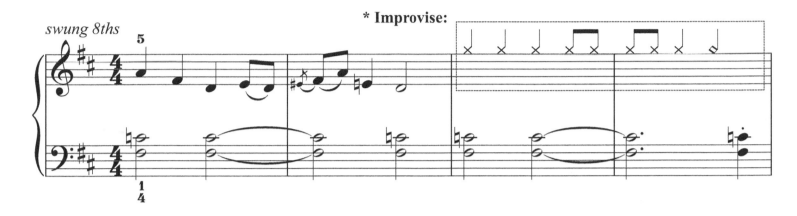

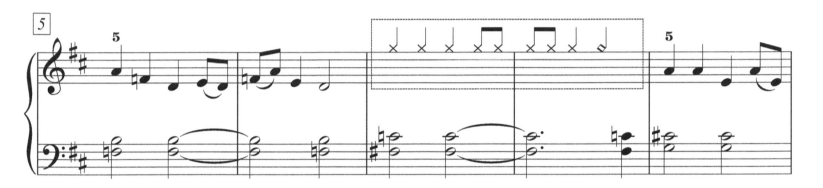

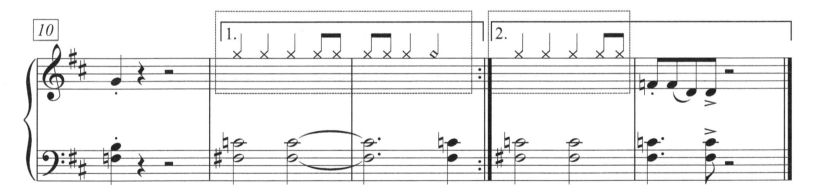

Listen closely as you play your improvisation.
 - Does each note sound good with the backing track?
 - Are you keeping a steady beat and staying with the backing track?
Play several different improvisations and choose your favorite. Play it for your teacher.

✔ **Improv Tip:** *The left hand ties create a syncopated effect that helps create momentum in the right hand.*
   Try to improvise a melody that has lots of energy!

Improv Etude - Boat Blues

MODULE 1

A Clap this rhythmic pattern with the backing track:

B Create your own RH melodies, as guided in steps 1-3.
Play without the backing track.
Where improv is indicated:

1. Use scale degree 1.
2. Use scale degrees 1 or 3.
3. Use scale degrees 1, 2, 3, 4, or 5.

C Repeat steps B1-3 with LH accompaniments.

1. Improvise on this rhythm using scale degrees 1, 2, 3, 4, or 5.

2. Improvise on this rhythm using scale degrees 1, 2, 3, 4, or 5.

3. Improvise on this rhythm using scale degrees 1, 2, 3, 4, or 5.

* Improv notes:

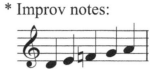

D Practice hands together with the backing track.
For mm. 1, 3, 5, 7, 9 & 11 improvise your own melodies
using the given rhythms and your ideas from step "C".

* **Improvise:**

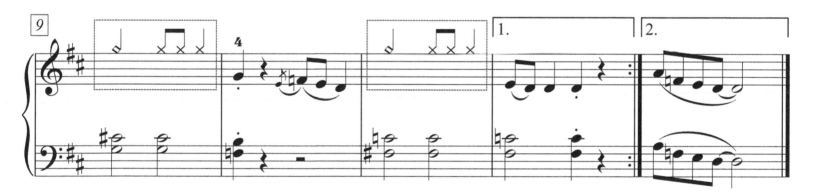

Listen closely as you play your improvisation.
- Does each note sound good with the backing track?
- Are you keeping a steady beat and staying with the backing track?
Play several different improvisations and choose your favorite. Play it for your teacher.

☑ **Improv Tip:** *You can begin your improvisation with just two - or even one! - notes.*
Then add more as you feel comfortable.

Improv Etude - Boat Blues

MODULE 2

A Clap this rhythmic pattern with the backing track:

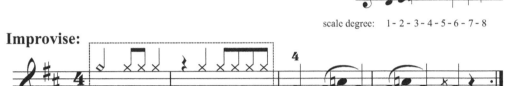

B Create your own RH melodies, as guided in steps 1-3.
Play without the backing track.
Where improv is indicated:

1. Use scale degree 1.
2. Use scale degrees 1 or 3.
3. Use scale degrees 1, 3, 4, 5, or 7.

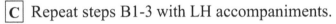

C Repeat steps B1-3 with LH accompaniments.

1. Improvise on this rhythm using scale degrees 1, 3, 4, 5, or 7.

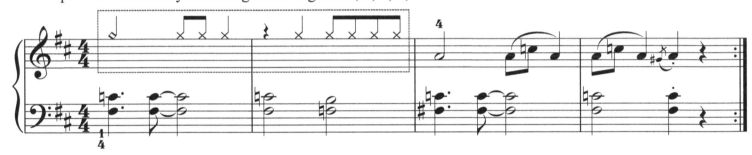

2. Improvise on this rhythm using scale degrees 1, 3, 4, 5, or 7.

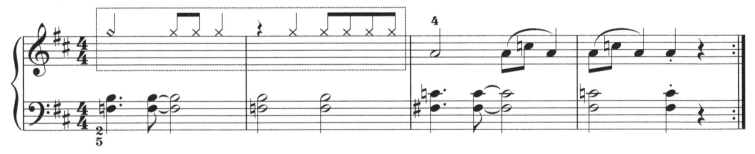

3. Improvise on this rhythm using scale degrees 2, 3, 4, 5, or 7.

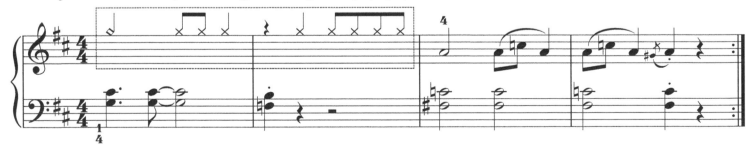

* Improv notes:

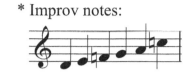

D Practice hands together with the backing track.
For mm. 1-2, 5-6 & 9-10 improvise your own melodies
using the given rhythms and your ideas from step "C".

* Improvise:

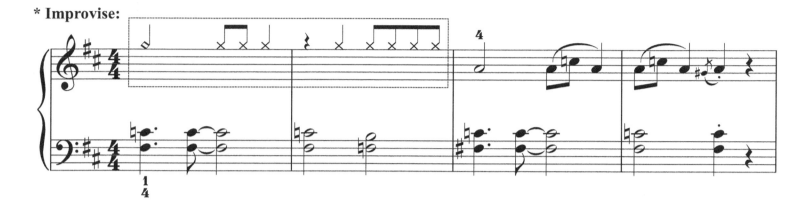

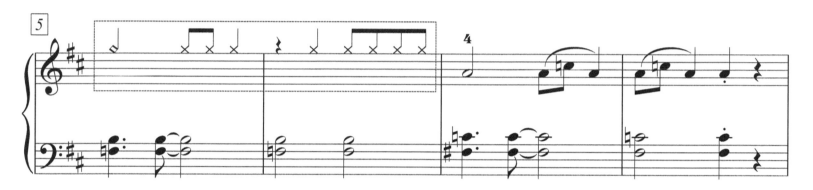

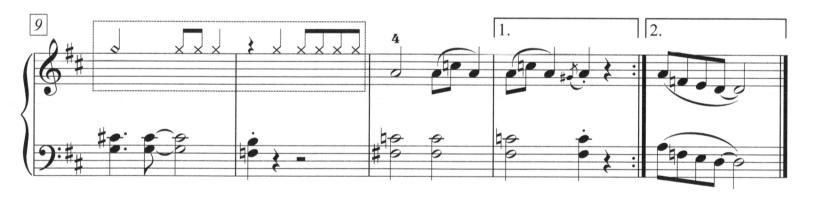

Listen closely as you play your improvisation.
- Does each note sound good with the backing track?
- Are you keeping a steady beat and staying with the backing track?
Play several different improvisations and choose your favorite. Play it for your teacher.

✔ **Improv Tip:** *The melody in mm. 4 & 12 uses a grace note to add musical interest.*
Try using grace notes in your improvisation to see when you like the sound!

Improv Etude - Boat Blues

MODULE 3

A Clap this rhythmic pattern with the backing track:

B Create your own RH melodies, as guided in steps 1-3.
Play without the backing track.
Where improv is indicated:

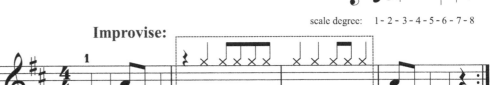

1. Use scale degree 1.
2. Use scale degrees 1 or 3.
3. Use scale degrees 1, 3,
   4, 5, or 7.

C Repeat steps B1-3 with LH accompaniments.

   1. Improvise on this rhythm using scale degrees 1, 3, 4, 5, or 7.

   2. Improvise on this rhythm using scale degrees 1, 3, 4, 5, or 7.

   3. Improvise on this rhythm using scale degrees 1, 3, 4, 5, or 7.

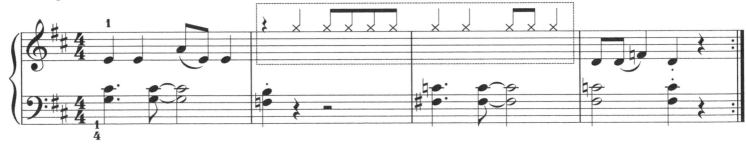

* Improv notes:

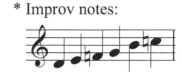

D Practice hands together with the backing track.
For mm. 2-3, 6-7 & 10-11 improvise your own melodies
using the given rhythms and your ideas from step "C".

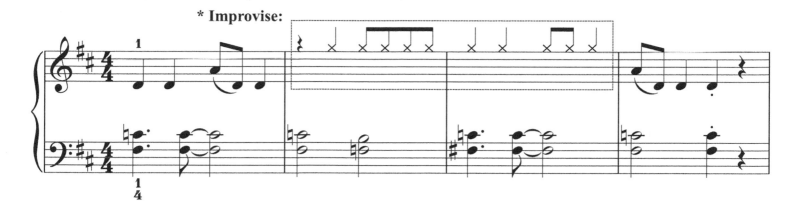

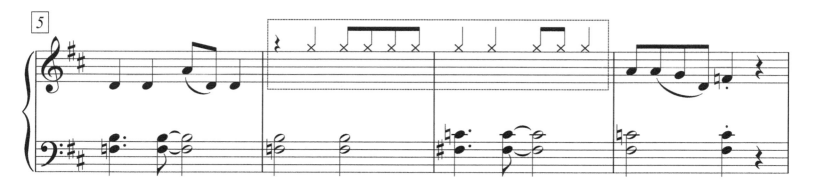

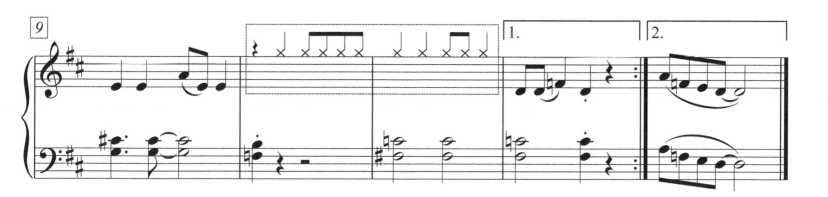

Listen closely as you play your improvisation.
- Does each note sound good with the backing track?
- Are you keeping a steady beat and staying with the backing track?
Play several different improvisations and choose your favorite. Play it for your teacher.

☑ **Improv Tip:** *Try repeating m. 1 in your improvisation.*
Where do you think it sounds best?

Improv Etude - Boat Blues

MODULE 4

A Clap this rhythmic pattern with the backing track:

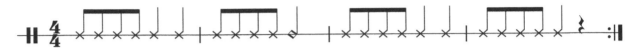

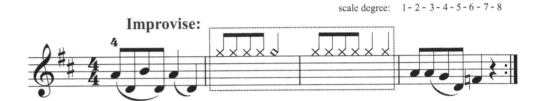

B Create your own RH melodies, as guided in steps 1-3.
Play without the backing track.
Where improv is indicated:

1. Use scale degree 1.
2. Use scale degrees 1 or 3.
3. Use scale degrees 1, 3,
   4, 5, 6, or 7.

C Repeat steps B1-3 with LH accompaniments.

1. Improvise on this rhythm using scale degrees 1, 3, 4, 5, 6, or 7.

2. Improvise on this rhythm using scale degrees 1, 3, 4, 5, 6, or 7.

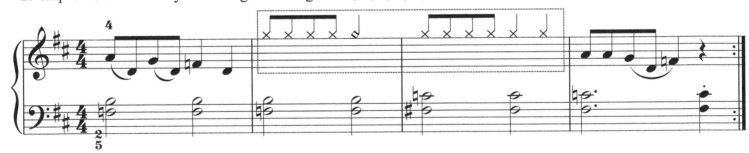

3. Improvise on this rhythm using scale degrees 1, 3, 4, 5, 6, or 7.

* Improv notes:

D Practice hands together with the backing track.
For mm. 2-3, 6-7 & 10-11 improvise your own melodies
using the given rhythms and your ideas from step "C".

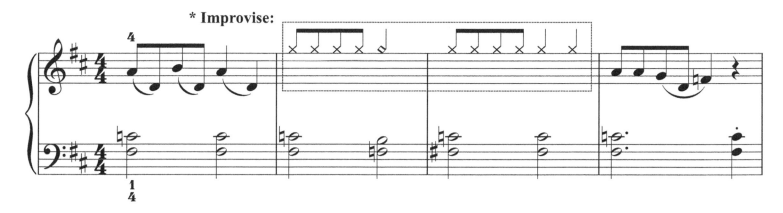

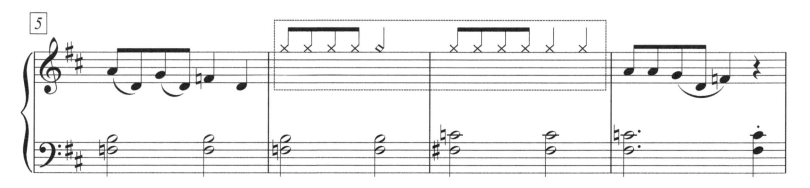

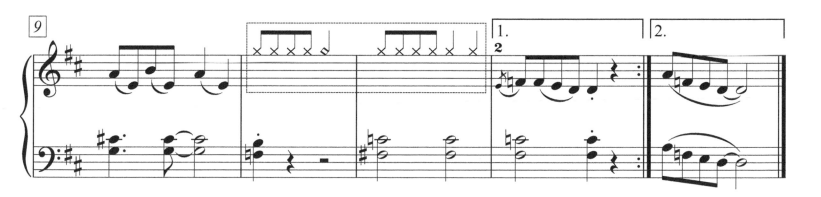

Listen closely as you play your improvisation.
- Does each note sound good with the backing track?
- Are you keeping a steady beat and staying with the backing track?
Play several different improvisations and choose your favorite. Play it for your teacher.

✔ **Improv Tip:** *The melody in m. 1 features two-note slurs - you can use these in your improvisation.*
Are there any slurs with more than two notes? Try using these, too!

Improv Etude - Family Holiday

MODULE 1

A Clap this rhythmic pattern with the backing track:

B Create your own RH melodies, as guided in steps 1-3.
Play without the backing track.
Where improv is indicated:

1. Use scale degree 1.
2. Use scale degrees 1 or 5.
3. Use scale degrees 1, 2, 3, 4, or 5.

C Repeat steps B1-3 with LH accompaniments.

    1. Improvise on this rhythm using scale degrees 1, 2, 3, 4, or 5.

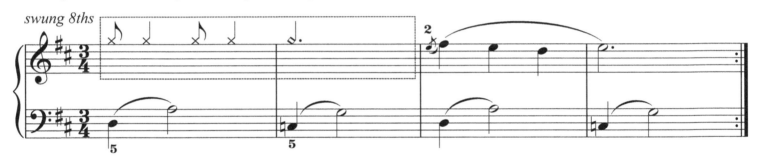

    2. Improvise on this rhythm using scale degrees 1, 2, 3, 4, or 5.

    3. Improvise on this rhythm using scale degrees 1, 2, 3, 4, or 5.

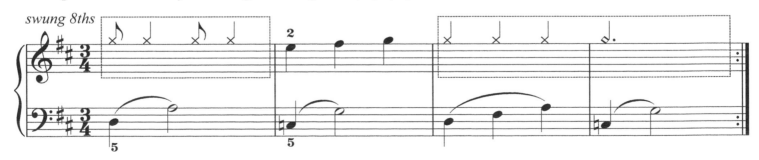

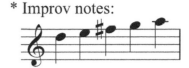

D Practice hands together with the backing track.
For mm. 1, 5, 7 & 9 improvise your own melodies
using the given rhythms and your ideas from step "C".

* Improvise:
swung 8ths

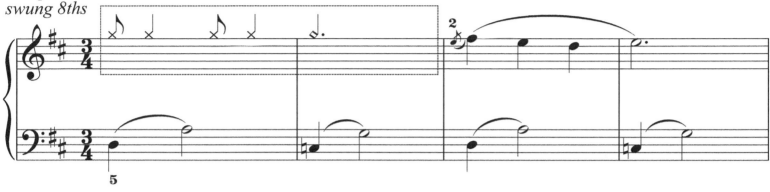

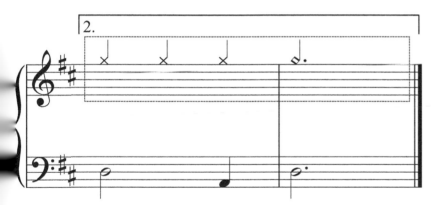

Listen closely as you play your improvisation.
- Does each note sound good with the backing track?
- Are you keeping a steady beat and staying with the backing track?

Play several different improvisations and choose your favorite. Play it for your teacher.

✔**Improv Tip:** *The Improv rhythm is exactly the same each time. Use at least one different note*
in each improv measure to make your improvisation more interesting!

Improv Etude - Family Holiday

MODULE 2

A Clap this rhythmic pattern with the backing track:

B Create your own RH melodies, as guided in steps 1-3.
Play without the backing track.
Where improv is indicated:

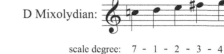

D Mixolydian:

scale degree: 7 - 1 - 2 - 3 - 4

1. Use scale degree 1.
2. Use scale degrees 1 or 2.
3. Use scale degrees 7, 1,
   2, 3, or 4.

Improvise:

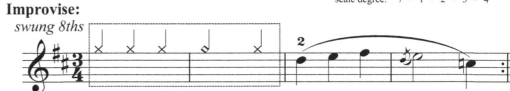

C Repeat steps B1-3 with LH accompaniments.

1. Improvise on this rhythm using scale degrees 7, 1, 2, 3, or 4.

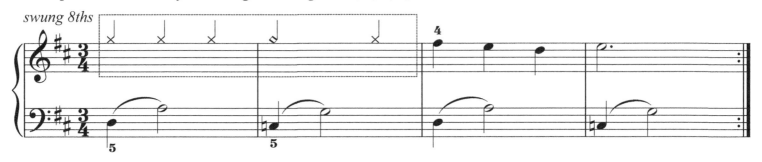

2. Improvise on this rhythm using scale degrees 7, 1, 2, 3, or 4.

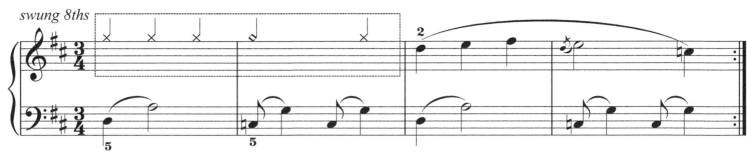

3. Improvise on this rhythm using scale degrees 7, 1, 2, 3, or 4.

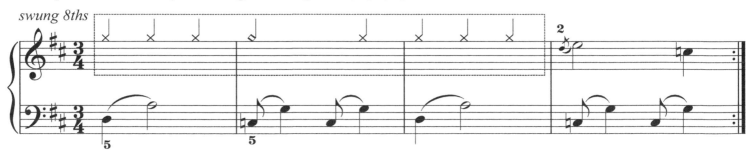

* Improv notes:

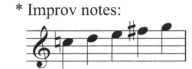

D Practice hands together with the backing track.
For mm. 1, 2, 5 & 6 improvise your own melodies
using the given rhythms and your ideas from step "C".

* Improvise:
swung 8ths

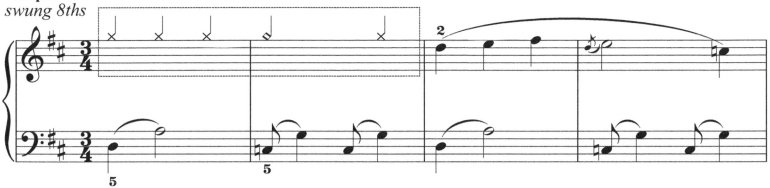

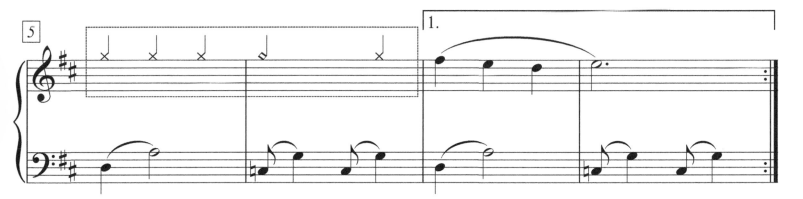

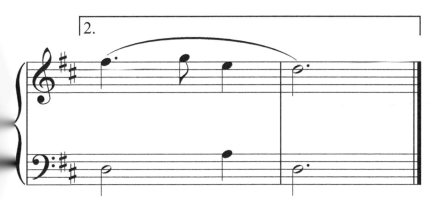

Listen closely as you play your improvisation.
- Does each note sound good with the backing track?
- Are you keeping a steady beat and staying with the backing track?
Play several different improvisations and choose your favorite. Play it for your teacher.

✔**Improv Tip:** *You could play scale patterns the first time, and then add chord tones on the repeat.*

Improv Etude - Family Holiday

MODULE 3

A Clap this rhythmic pattern with the backing track:

B Create your own RH melodies, as guided in steps 1-3.
Play without the backing track.
Where improv is indicated:

1. Use scale degree 1.
2. Use scale degrees 1 or 2.
3. Use scale degrees 1, 2, 3, 4, or 5.

C Repeat steps B1-3 with LH accompaniments.

1. Improvise on this rhythm using scale degrees 7, 1, 2, 3, 4, or 5.

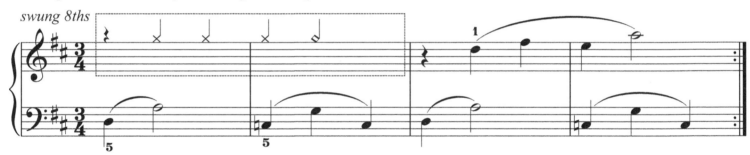

2. Improvise on this rhythm using scale degrees 7, 1, 2, 3, 4, or 5.

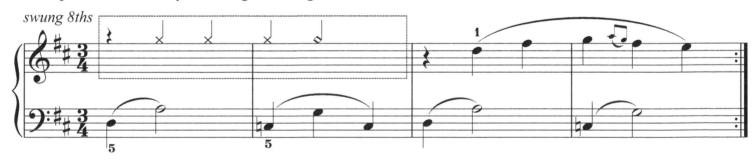

3. Improvise on this rhythm using scale degrees 7, 1, 2, 3, 4, or 5.

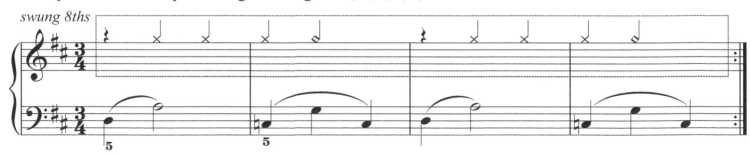

* Improv notes:

D Practice hands together with the backing track.
For mm. 1, 2, 5, 6, 7 & 8 improvise your own melodies
using the given rhythms and your ideas from step "C".

* Improvise:
swung 8ths

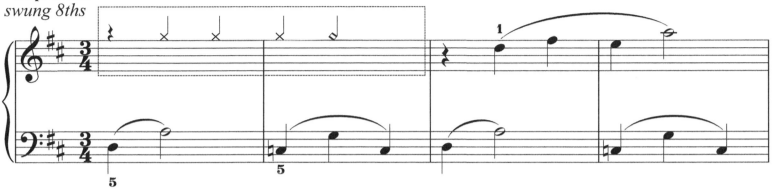

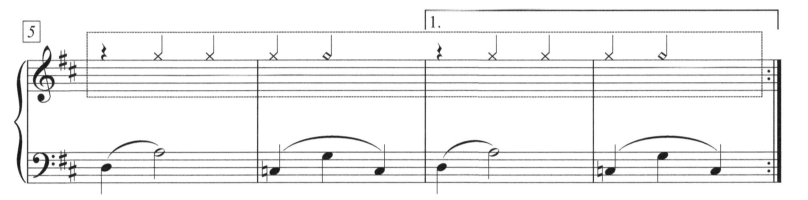

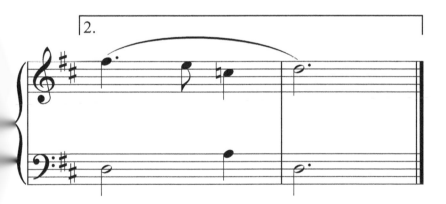

Listen closely as you play your improvisation.
- Does each note sound good with the backing track?
- Are you keeping a steady beat and staying with the backing track?
Play several different improvisations and choose your favorite. Play it for your teacher.

✔ **Improv Tip:** *Because the right hand has fewer notes to play, be more daring and
experimental about what order you play them in.*

Improv Etude - Family Holiday

MODULE 4

A Clap this rhythmic pattern with the backing track:

B Create your own RH melodies, as guided in steps 1-3.
Play without the backing track.
Where improv is indicated:

1. Use scale degree 1.
2. Use scale degrees 1 or 2.
3. Use scale degrees 1, 2, 3, 4, or 5.

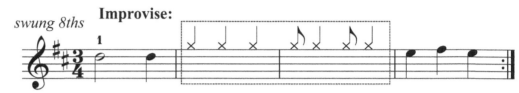

C Repeat steps B1-3 with LH accompaniments.

1. Improvise on this rhythm using scale degrees 7, 1, 2, 3, 4, or 5.

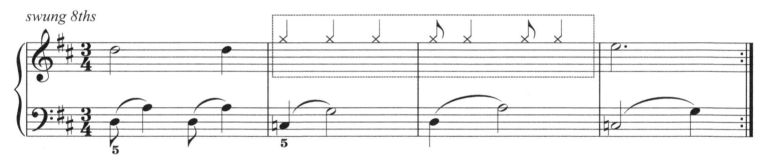

2. Improvise on this rhythm using scale degrees 7, 1, 2, 3, 4, or 5.

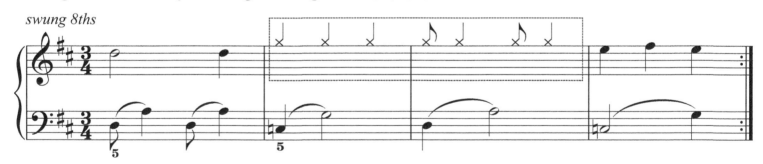

3. Improvise on this rhythm using scale degrees 7, 1, 2, 3, 4, or 5.

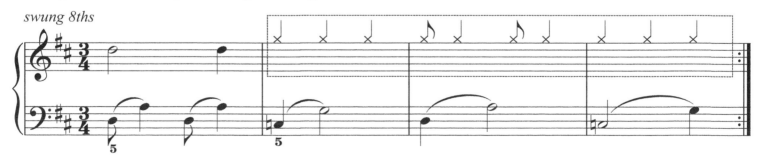

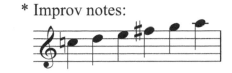

* Improv notes:

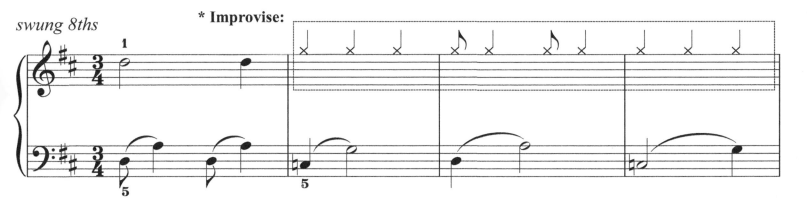

D Practice hands together with the backing track.
For mm. 2, 3, 4, 6 & 7 improvise your own melodies
using the given rhythms and your ideas from step "C".

swung 8ths

* **Improvise:**

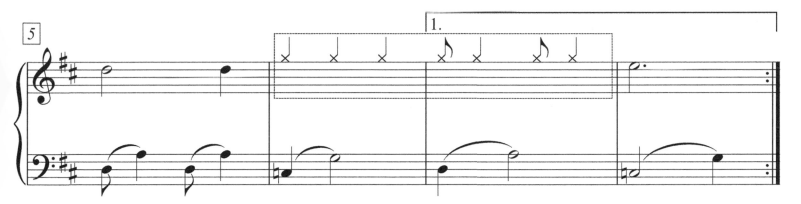

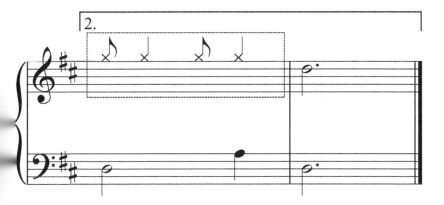

Listen closely as you play your improvisation.
- Does each note sound good with the backing track?
- Are you keeping a steady beat and staying with the backing track?
Play several different improvisations and choose your favorite. Play it for your teacher.

✔**Improv Tip:** *Have you figured out what chords are implied by the accompaniment?*
Use these as the basis for your improvisation.

Improv Etude - Spider Blues

MODULE 1

A Clap this rhythmic pattern with the backing track:

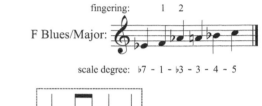

B Create your own RH melodies, as guided in steps 1-3.
Play without the backing track.
Where improv is indicated:

1. Use scale degree 1.
2. Use scale degrees 1 or 5.
3. Use scale degrees 1, ♭3, 3, 4, or 5.

C Repeat steps B1-3 with LH accompaniments.

   1. Improvise on this rhythm using scale degrees 1, ♭3, 3, 4, or 5.

   2. Improvise on this rhythm using scale degrees 1, ♭3, 3, 4, or 5.

   3. Improvise on this rhythm using scale degrees 1, ♭3, 3, 4, or 5.

* Improv notes:

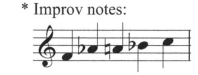

D Practice hands together with the backing track.
For mm. 1, 3, 5, 7, 9 & 11 improvise your own melodies
using the given rhythms and your ideas from step "C".

* Improvise:

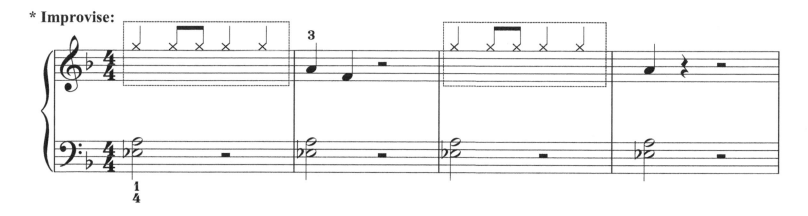

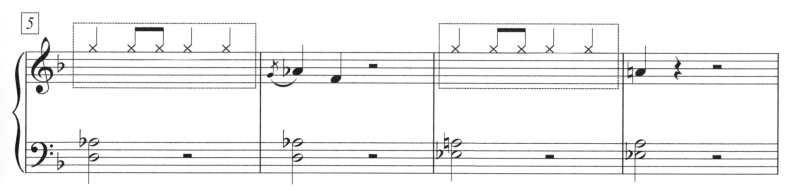

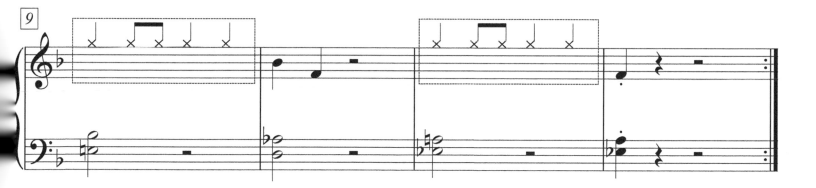

Listen closely as you play your improvisation.
- Does each note sound good with the backing track?
- Are you keeping a steady beat and staying with the backing track?
Play several different improvisations and choose your favorite. Play it for your teacher.

✔ **Improv Tip:** *Your improvisation can use either A♭ or A♮ - more blues notes!*

Improv Etude - Spider Blues

MODULE 2

A Clap this rhythmic pattern with the backing track:

B Create your own RH melodies, as guided in steps 1-3.
Play without the backing track.
Where improv is indicated:

1. Use scale degree 1.
2. Use scale degrees 1 or ♭3.
3. Use scale degrees ♭7, 1, ♭3, 3, or 4.

C Repeat steps B1-3 with LH accompaniments.

1. Improvise on this rhythm using scale degrees ♭7, 1, ♭3, 3, or 4.

2. Improvise on this rhythm using scale degrees ♭7, 1, ♭3, 3, or 4.

3. Improvise on this rhythm using scale degrees ♭7, 1, ♭3, 3, or 4.

* Improv notes:

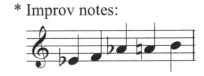

D Practice hands together with the backing track.
For mm. 1, 3, 5, 7, 9 & 11 improvise your own melodies
using the given rhythms and your ideas from step "C".

* **Improvise:**

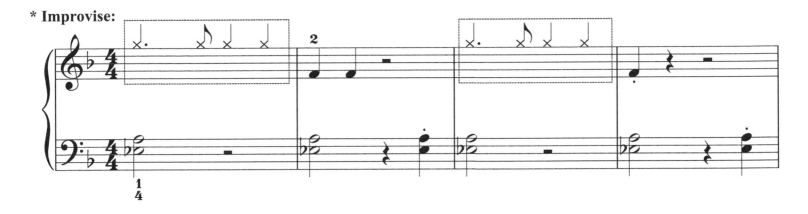

Listen closely as you play your improvisation.
- Does each note sound good with the backing track?
- Are you keeping a steady beat and staying with the backing track?
Play several different improvisations and choose your favorite. Play it for your teacher.

✔ **Improv Tip:** *A right hand melody in F pentatonic minor - F, A♭, B♭, (C), E♭ - will work in F Blues!*
Try using only these notes in your improvisation.

Improv Etude - Spider Blues

MODULE 3

A Clap this rhythmic pattern with the backing track:

B Create your own RH melodies, as guided in steps 1-3.
Play without the backing track.
Where improv is indicated:

1. Use scale degree 1.
2. Use scale degrees ♭7 or 1.
3. Use scale degrees ♭7, 1, ♭3, 3, or 4.

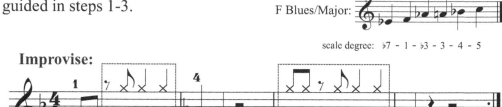

C Repeat steps B1-3 with LH accompaniments.

1. Improvise on this rhythm using scale degrees ♭7, 1, ♭3, 3, or 4.

2. Improvise on this rhythm using scale degrees ♭7, 1, ♭3, 3, or 4.

3. Improvise on this rhythm using scale degrees ♭7, 1, ♭3, 3, or 4.

* Improv notes:

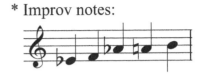

D Practice hands together with the backing track.
For mm. 1, 3, 5, 7, 9 & 11 improvise your own melodies
using the given rhythms and your ideas from step "C".

* **Improvise:**

Listen closely as you play your improvisation.
- Does each note sound good with the backing track?
- Are you keeping a steady beat and staying with the backing track?
Play several different improvisations and choose your favorite. Play it for your teacher.

☑ **Improv Tip:** *Notice how this written melody uses the same rhythmic figure throughout and varies the notes.*
What notes do you want to try in your improvisation?

Improv Etude - Spider Blues

MODULE 4

A Clap this rhythmic pattern with the backing track:

B Create your own RH melodies, as guided in steps 1-3.
Play without the backing track.
Where improv is indicated:

1. Use scale degree 1.
2. Use scale degrees 1 or ♭3.
3. Use scale degrees 1, ♭3, 3, 4, or 5.

Improvise:

C Repeat steps B1-3 with LH accompaniments.

1. Improvise on this rhythm using scale degrees 1, ♭3, 3, 4, or 5.

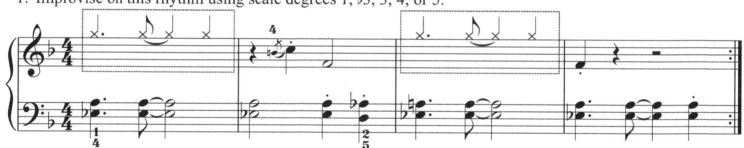

2. Improvise on this rhythm using scale degrees 1, ♭3, 3, 4, or 5.

3. Improvise on this rhythm using scale degrees 1, ♭3, 3, 4, or 5.

* Improv notes:

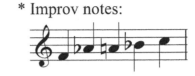

D Practice hands together with the backing track.
For mm. 1, 3, 5, 7, 9 & 11 improvise your own melodies
using the given rhythms and your ideas from step "C".

* **Improvise:**

Listen closely as you play your improvisation.
- Does each note sound good with the backing track?
- Are you keeping a steady beat and staying with the backing track?
Play several different improvisations and choose your favorite. Play it for your teacher.

✔ **Improv Tip:** *Experiment with adding grace notes in different places.*

Performance Etude - War Dance

A Practice the *War Dance* Performance Etude based on
the notes and rhythms you have already used in the modules.
Once this feels comfortable, experiment with your own rhythms.
Do this several times.

B Work on your improvisation without the backing track until you can play with a steady tempo.
Then practice with the backing track. Choose your favorite version and play it for your teacher.

Listen closely as you play your improvisation.
- Does each note sound good with the backing track?
- Are you keeping a steady beat and staying with the backing track?

✔ **Improv Tip:** *Try to have the melody in your mind before you play it.*

Performance Etude - Celtic Caper

A Practice the *Celtic Caper* Performance Etude based on
the notes and rhythms you have already used in the modules.
Once this feels comfortable, experiment with your own rhythms.
Do this several times.

B Work on your improvisation without the backing track until you can play with a steady tempo.
Then practice with the backing track. Choose your favorite version and play it for your teacher.

Listen closely as you play your improvisation.
- Does each note sound good with the backing track?
- Are you keeping a steady beat and staying with the backing track?

✔ **Improv Tip:** *Try copying the rhythm of the given melody, then create a completely different rhythm.*

Performance Etude - KC Shuffle

A Practice the *KC Shuffle* Performance Etude based on the notes and rhythms you have already used in the modules. Once this feels comfortable, experiment with your own rhythms. Do this several times.

Improv notes:

B Work on your improvisation without the backing track until you can play with a steady tempo. Then practice with the backing track. Choose your favorite version and play it for your teacher.

Listen closely as you play your improvisation.
- Does each note sound good with the backing track?
- Are you keeping a steady beat and staying with the backing track?

✔ **Improv Tip:** *Vary your right hand's rhythms - but not too much. Repetition of patterns is important.*

Performance Etude - Boat Blues

A Practice the *Boat Blues* Performance Etude based on the notes and rhythms you have already used in the modules. Once this feels comfortable, experiment with your own rhythms. Do this several times.

Improv notes:

B Work on your improvisation without the backing track until you can play with a steady tempo. Then practice with the backing track. Choose your favorite version and play it for your teacher.

Toot that horn

Listen closely as you play your improvisation.
- Does each note sound good with the backing track?
- Are you keeping a steady beat and staying with the backing track?

✔ **Improv Tip:** *Try to be varied in your improvisation -*
different note values, silences, repetition ... be creative!

Performance Etude - Family Holiday

A Practice the *Family Holiday* Performance Etude based on
the notes and rhythms you have already used in the modules.
Once this feels comfortable, experiment with your own rhythms.
Do this several times.

Improv notes:

B Work on your improvisation without the backing track until you can play with a steady tempo.
Then practice with the backing track. Choose your favorite version and play it for your teacher.

Listen closely as you play your improvisation.
- Does each note sound good with the backing track?
- Are you keeping a steady beat and staying with the backing track?

✔ Improv Tip: *Notice how using different registers creates a very different expressive effect.*

Performance Etude - Spider Blues

A Practice the *Spider Blues* Performance Etude based on
the notes and rhythms you have already used in the modules.
Once this feels comfortable, experiment with your own rhythms.
Do this several times.

Improv notes:

B Work on your improvisation without the backing track until you can play with a steady tempo.
Then practice with the backing track. Choose your favorite version and play it for your teacher.

Driving

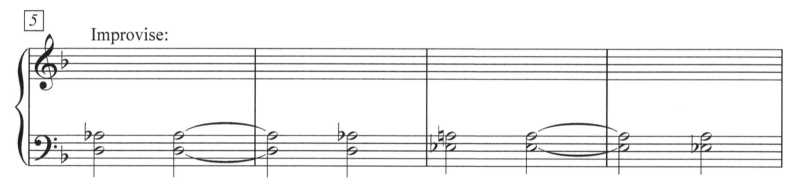

Listen closely as you play your improvisation.
- Does each note sound good with the backing track?
- Are you keeping a steady beat and staying with the backing track?

✔ **Improv Tip:** *The hands don't need to be together rhymically.*
In fact, the more rhythmic interplay between them, the better.

Allegro

F. Beyer

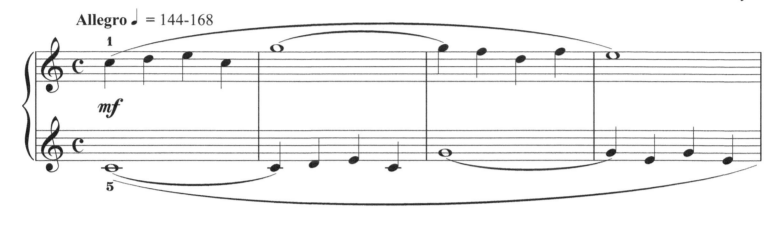

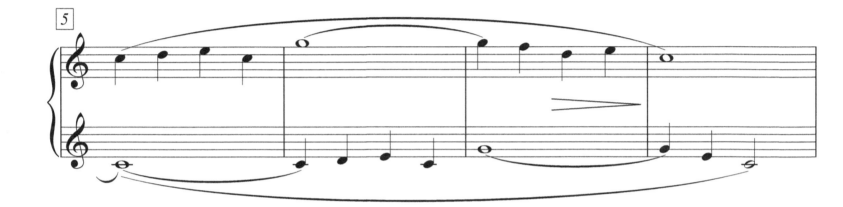

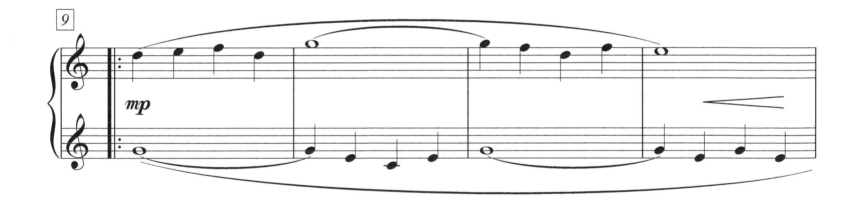

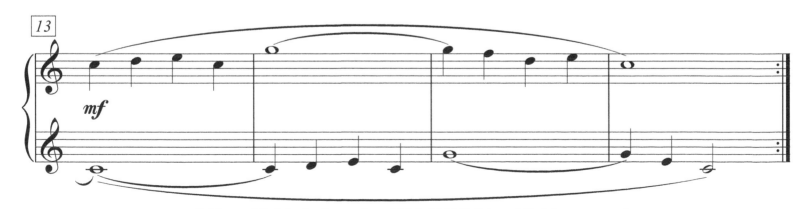

Allegretto

C. Gurlitt

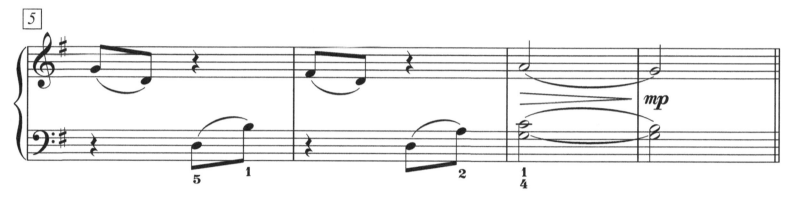

Swedish Dance

H. Berens

Allegretto

L. Kohler

Moderato

F. Beyer

Andante Op. 14 no. 14

K. M. Kunz

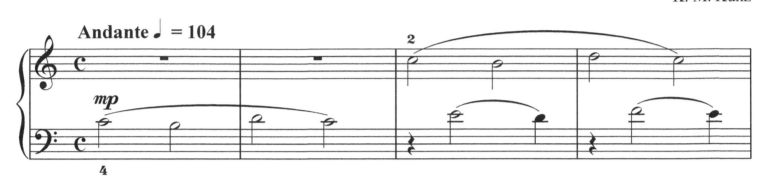

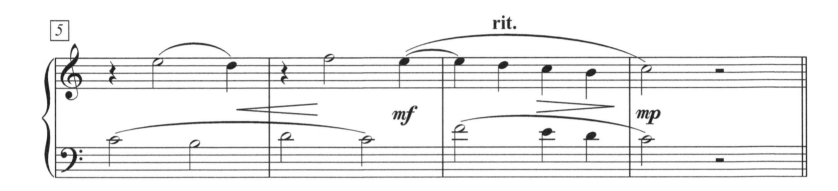

Allegretto

F. Le Couppey

Moderato

Ludvig Schytte

Allegro

C. Czerny

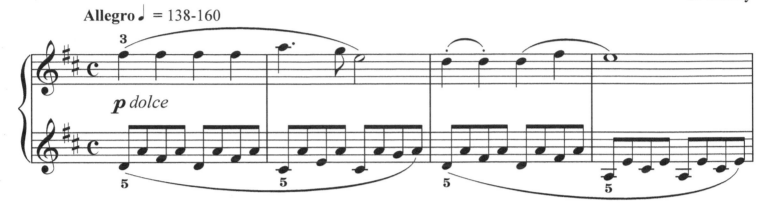

Talking Point

Christopher Norton

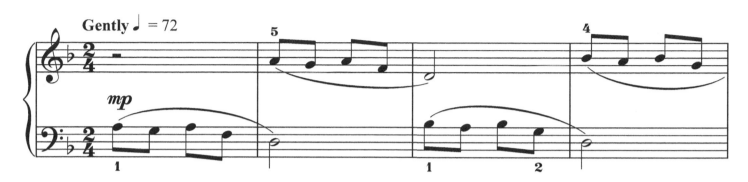

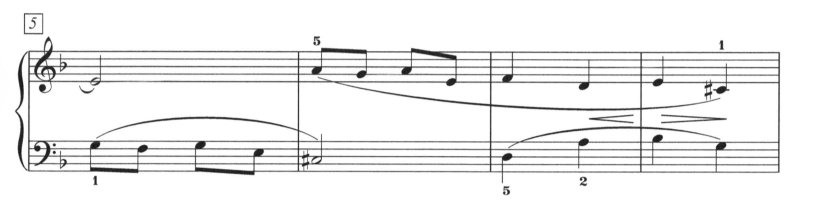

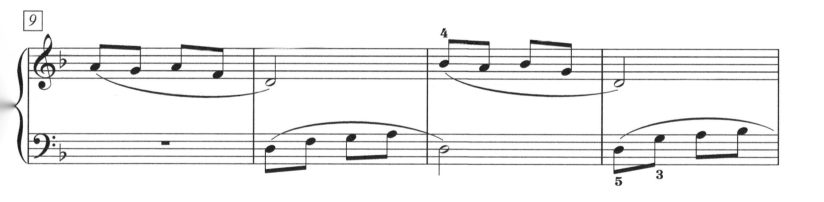

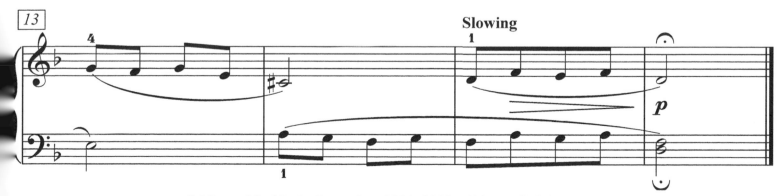

Rocknophobic

Christopher Norton

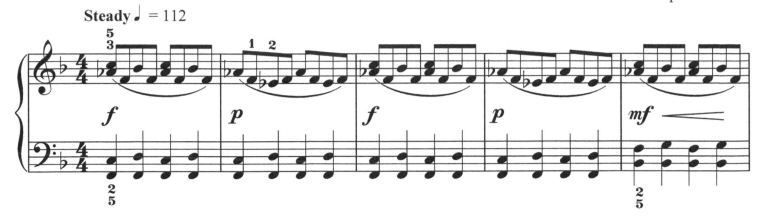

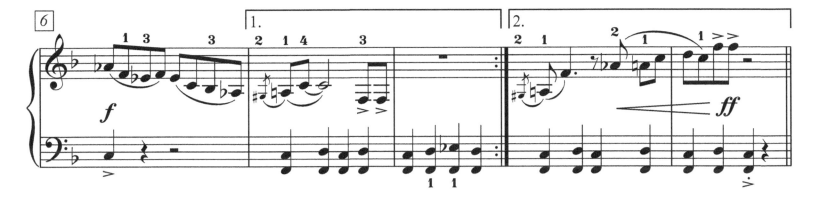

Bubble Wrap

Christopher Norton

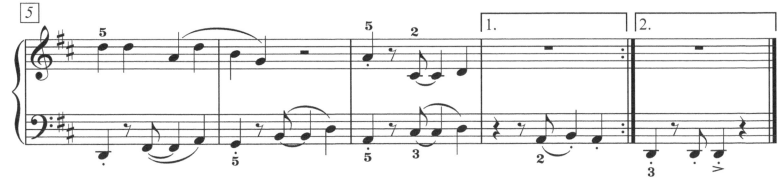

In The Shadows

Mysteriously ♩ = 112

Christopher Norton

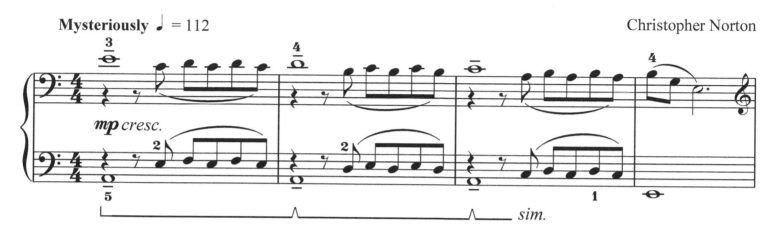

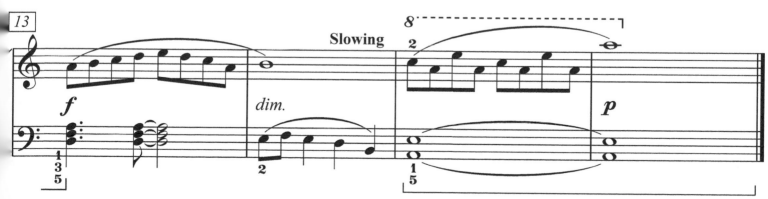

Waterlilies

Christopher Norton

Little Blues

Christopher Norton

Spelunking

Christopher Norton

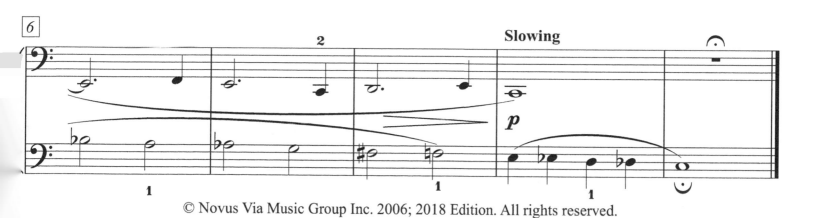

Out For The Evening

Christopher Norton

Jolly ♩ = 120-132

Ring Dance

Christopher Norton

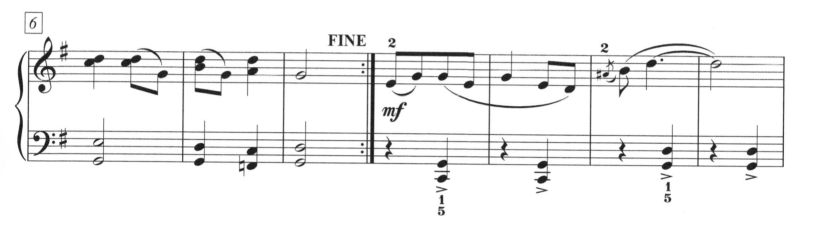

D.C. al fine

LEVEL ③ ETUDES
Glossary

Symbols

♪ .... **Grace note** a note printed in small size, always played quickly in pop music.

⌒ ...... **Slur** play the notes under or over the slur legato. Sometimes, the last note of a slur is shortened a bit.

Staccato one or more notes that are detached from other notes, and released quickly.

Tenuto has two meanings:
1) emphasize the note a little bit;
2) hold the note for its full length, without connecting it to the following note. It could have either or both meanings–it is up to the performer to decide.

Terms and Forms

Accompaniment The part of a piece that provides musical background for the melody.

a tempo .... Return to the original tempo.

Blues........... Musical genre created by African-American musicians, with "blues" notes played against a major-key chord progression. Examples include: *Spider Blues, Heartbreak Hotel*

Blues notes .... A pattern based on a major scale with lowered 3rd, 5th, and 7th notes.

Bossa nova .... A Brazilian dance style, with a 2+3+3 eighth note pattern in the right hand over a dotted quarter note, eighth note pattern in the left hand, often with rich, sensuous chords. Examples include: *End of a Lovely Day, Desifinado*

Call and response .... A style of singing in which the melody sung by one singer is echoed or "answered" by another. Examples include: *My Generation*

Calypso........ A popular song form from the Caribbean island of Trinidad, generally upbeat. Examples include: *Yellow Bird*

Cha cha .... An exciting syncopated Latin dance, with a characteristic "cha cha cha" rhythm at the end. Examples include: *Never on a Sunday*

Coda .... "Tail". In music, it means an ending section.

Country Swing . A combination of country, cowboy, polka, and folk music, blended with a jazzy "swing", featuring pedal steel guitar. Examples include: *Country Boy, Lovesick Blues* (Hank Williams)

Da Capo (D.C.). "The head". It means go back to the beginning and play again.

Dal segno (D.S.) "From the sign". Look for the 𝄋 sign and repeat from that spot.

Fanfare......... A loud flourish of brass instruments, especially trumpets. Examples include: *Fanfare, Fanfare for the Common Man*

Fine .... End.

Form .... The arrangement of patterns in a piece, often based on repetition. **ABA** a three-part form. The first section repeats at the end, with a contrasted section in the middle.

Gospel .... An African-American religious style featuring a solo singer with heavily ornamented, simple melodies and a dramatic wide vocal range. The soloist is often accompanied by a choir providing a rich harmonic backdrop. Examples include: *Nobody Knows the Trouble I've Seen*

Interval .... The distance from one note to another. **Harmonic intervals** two notes played at the same time. **Melodic intervals** two notes played one after the other.

Irish Jig .... A lively dance in triple time, generally led by tin whistle and fiddle. Examples include: *Celtic Caper, The Rambler*

Jazz waltz...... A generally relaxed swing style in 3/4 time. Examples include: *My Favorite Things*

Legato .... Smooth and connected.

loco .... Return to normal position.

Motif.......... A musical idea. It may consist of a short melody, a short rhythmic pattern, or both.

Motown........ A style of music which originated in Detroit, whose features include the use of tambourine along with drums and a "call and response" singing style derived from gospel music. Examples include: *Motor City, ABC*

Off-beat........ An accented note, motif, or phrase played on a normally unaccented beat.

Reggae......... A music style from Jamaica, with elements of calypso, rhythm and blues, and characterized by a strong offbeat. Examples include: *Jamaican Market, No Woman No Cry*

Rhythm and blues .... A style of music that combines blues and jazz, characterized by a strong off-beat and variations on syncopated instrumental phrases.

Sopra........... "Over". Usually used to indicate which hand plays over top of the other in a crossed-hands section.

Subito.......... Suddenly.

Shuffle......... Named after the tap dancing style where the dancer, wearing soft-soled shoes, "shuffles" their feet in a swung 8ths rhythm. Examples include: *KC Shuffle, All Shook Up*

Soul .... An African-American style combining elements of gospel music and rhythm and blues.

Swing.......... A fun, dance-like style, usually using swung 8ths.

Swung 8ths .... 8th notes that are written normally, but played in this gentle dotted rhythm:

Syncopation ... An emphasis on weak beats and/or rests on strong beats to briefly change the pattern of metrical accents normally found in a time signature. This word is sometimes used to mean "offbeat".

Tango .... A rhythmically strict style, with no off-beat and a snare roll on beat 4. Examples include: *Tango of the Desert, Don't Cry for Me Argentina*

Tone cluster ... A dissonant group of two or more closely spaced notes sounded at the same time.

Waltz........... A dance in 3/4 time, usually played with a strong accent on the first beat, with weaker beats on counts 2 and 3 in the accompaniment. Examples include: *Doleful, Edelweiss*